I0421710

THE
BREXIT
INDECISION

The conflicting views of one man in the lead up to the Brexit vote

Edward Taylor

Published in the United Kingdom of Great Britain and Northern Ireland

First published online in May 2016

Amended and published in print in 2019

ISBN: 978 1 070 67893 1

H M T Q

Contents

Introduction

The United Kingdom's referendum on European Union membership in 2016 split the kingdom down the middle. The infamous result, 52%-48% is often said to have given *Brexit* the largest popular mandate of any vote in the United Kingdom.

Prior to the vote in 2016. The largest popular mandate has been the election of the Tory party led by John Major in 1992, with 14,093,007 votes. But after 23rd June, that languished in third place behind the vote to leave the EU (new champion, 17,410,742 votes) and the vote to remain (new second place, 16,141,241 votes).

The debates within the UK are well documented and have raged ever since. They have consumed British politics like a parasite, slowly feeding on political will and energy at the expense of more worthy causes. The United Kingdom found itself in a trap of its own making, unable to decide how to escape.

Less well documented are the debates within people, those who, like the kingdom itself, found their sympathies were split, 52%-48%, down the middle. Whilst decisions were often loud and vocal, the decision-making processes were often silent and personal.

It is this process that we shall try and understand here, by examining the thoughts of one individual, who considered the many facets of this complex decision. Leave or remain? Remain or leave? So much hinged on the precise placement of that × on that summer day in 2016.

So it is that we introduce our 35-year-old voter. He lives in a commuter town in East Anglia. He has recently bought a house. He is university educated. He is employed, for which he travels into London every day. He is comfortable. Of the 33,577,342 votes cast in the referendum, one was his.

His political affiliations have changed over the years; he has voted Liberal, Tory and Labour. When studying A-Levels in the late 1990s, he was very politically aware and staunchly pro-European. His Europhilia did not survive the Blair years.

What makes this one man special, what makes him the subject of this modest tome, is his private note-taking leading up to the 2016 plebiscite. It is a collection of personal notes, written for the purpose of helping him decide which way to vote one month thereafter.

We can know his thoughts, his priorities. What lies did he believe? What did he know? What did he think he knew? What did he think was simple? What did he worry about?

So, let's see what he had to say about Brexit during the dawn of national polarisation, before his views were corrupted by hindsight.

£350 Million a Week

Leave

Red buses notwithstanding, obviously, we pay more into the EU than we get out of it. So, all subsidies could remain in place and we'll have £8 billion surplus/year and all those developments won't have to have the EU flag all over the place making it look like a gift we didn't actually pay for.

Farming subsidies, research subsidies, everything in this country that the EU pays for can be paid for and still we have £8,000,000,000+ a year back. That's a lot.

Remain

But I'm not convinced that we are able to allocate this money to any one area. For all the headline-grabbing talk about extra funding for the NHS, we might need that money as a buffer against any new trade tariffs and the resulting economic shock of an exit. Non-EU organisations which get EU funding will probably require we pick up the slack if we want to remain a member, organisations such as the European Space Agency. Or is the proposal that we leave those sorts of things too?

My concern here is that the subsidies are currently spent in rather good areas and the general inability of the EU to make decisions and change probably means it'll be like this for a while.

If we leave, they'll probably be unchanged in the short term, but will Westminster, Holyrood *etc* keep them in the long term? I somehow doubt it. The temptation to give the farmers a little less and the NHS a little more will probably be too much, especially during a hard-fought election campaign.

But at least if the NHS needs a little more, we can make that decision if we leave. I might not trust Westminster's decisions, but I still think it should be their decision (and appropriately devolved) and the fact that we get an extra £8 billion on top of the decision-making power really makes me think we should leave. Even the woefully inefficient Westminster government must be able to do some good with that, even if it is poured into the national debt.

I don't believe the bus. I know what the figures are and that £350 million a week is a very selective choice of figure. The question is, what other lies are the leave campaign telling me?

British Influence in Europe

Leave

Remain

Britain being in the EU influences EU decisions for the benefit of everyone.

Maybe.

Following a fatal coach crash caused by old tyres, a (pro-EU) MP wanted to ban tyres over a certain age from being legally used on public vehicles. I believe the ban was approved by the House of Commons.

He then took it to Brussels to roll the ban out EU-wide. But they just didn't want to know. It was an utter snub.

When an elected representative of the British people goes with a message akin to "we've done this, you might want to too", and they don't give him the time of day, our influence can't be that great now can it?

But international influence is a quiet beast, we might have been the most instrumental force in EU policy for all we know. Such policies do not tend to say "made in England" on them.

But look at what we do know. Our policy and suggestion to take the neediest Syrian refugees from the camps in the Middle East, rather than the free-for-all, people smuggler-friendly policy of Angela Merkel, was ignored.

British influence in Europe's council of ministers is only 8%.

Our influence hasn't stopped the EU from going from crisis to crisis. Our influence has not gotten the EU to scrap the *Tampon Tax*. We are currently trying to exercise our influence to get an EU ban on microplastics in soaps and toothpaste, which are an easily solvable source of ocean pollution, to no avail. The government is talking

about a unilateral UK ban since EU support just isn't forthcoming.

This shows how limited our influence really
is.

So, we've had some debates and lost. So,
we're only one part of a large continent. So,
things move slowly in the EU. All of this
does not make our influence any greater if
we leave.

If we leave, our influence will be zero, or
at least only as influential as the next non-
EU country.

We might lament the EU's sluggishness
and inefficiency, but nowhere here is there
a reason to leave.

Fishing

Leave

The common fisheries policy has destroyed fish stocks and contributed to the decline of our fishing industry by allocating British territorial waters to other nations.

Norway and Iceland have preserved their fish stocks far more successfully.

Remain

Norway's healthy fish stocks is but one example. A common fisheries policy can preserve fish stocks for the future far more effectively than individual nations. By a joined-up approach, the EU can preserve stocks far greater than a disjointed nationalistic approach.

But it doesn't work like that. The common fisheries policy is at best an example of the road to hell being paved with good intentions. Good in principle, devastating and catastrophic in practice.

The reality is much worse than that, and is instead a classic example of how the EU is really a vehicle for national self-interest.

They saw four countries with large fish stocks and territorial waters lining up to join the EEC and they rushed through the Common Fisheries Policy, knowing that if it was passed before the new members joined, they would just have to accept it how it is. It was a massive territory grab. Three of those countries, the UK, Ireland and Denmark, fell for it. The fourth, Norway, turned and ran.

The history of the policy is not important. Its potential is, and it has potential.

But that potential is so far flung that it can be discounted. The potential is also limited. The EU does not own vast sea migration routes around us, its territory ends at Scotland. The rest is essentially lawless inter-national waters.

The same might not be said of the Med-iterranean…

…but Gibraltar's territorial waters are such a tiny slither that such reasoning hardly holds sway there. We shall never obstruct Cypriot policy or regulations off Akrotiri or Dhekelia.

But even within the EU's waters, there is no sign of anything becoming joined-up or the policy being utilised in an environ-mentally friendly way.

Dead fish are dumped overboard so more profitable fish can be caught within quota. It has institutionalised waste. It is still a nationalist land-grab. It is despicable.

Security

Leave

Remain

Security cooperation with other EU states means we're safer inside the bloc.

I think this is probably correct…

…but doubt that cooperation will stop if we leave. We coordinate security with many other countries, and to a greater extent than with our EU partners.

The inability to stop EU passport holders from entering the country is a security-related argument to leave. We have no control over who Latvia issues citizenship to, yet we have to let them into the UK in any event.

Unless we can prove that they pose a risk to the UK…

…which is a lengthy process.

I can nit-pick the minutia of security concerns, but in the end I have to rely on the experts on this one, and conclude that it is better for our security if we remain.

But EU security has proven woefully inadequate in Belgium, so I do tend to put more trust in the British security services than the rest of Europe combined. The British security services are, if we leave, leaving with us.

But those British security services, in which I have so much trust, tell me that it is more secure, it is safer, to stay.

Democracy

Leave

I elect an MP. Or more accurately, I get outvoted and other people elect my MP. She is my representative in parliament. If I am aggrieved, I can go to her, she can petition the relevant minister and that minister can overrule a poor decision.

But the minister is powerless to intervene if the matter is controlled by Europe.

If I don't like a law, and enough other people don't like it, the government can be voted out through our relatively crooked democracy, and the new government can repeal the law. But they are powerless to repeal EU laws. They could introduce a law which would overrule an EU law, were it not for the fact that EU law is senior to our law.

At this most basic level, our national democracy is a semi-devolved entity subject to EU control, which can override it on any matter regardless of national mood.

Remain

But I also elect an MEP through a somewhat fairer system than I elect my MP. Or to be even more accurate, I elect my MEPs, as I don't have just one representative but many.

My MEP choice is restricted to the party lists, I do not vote for a single individual whose opinions are akin to mine. I vote for a party, so could simultaneously vote for candidates who are aligned with my views and opposed to them. This in itself dilutes the democracy.

The single choice per party in UK elections gives me very little more choice in that regard either. And I can check who is top of the party list.

The democratic deficit must be compared with the one we would have if we leave, rather than an ideal democracy, if there is such a thing.

My MEPs are my representatives and they are democratically elected, they can collectively veto any new law. They approve nominations to the European Commission too.

But to take the previous example of a law I don't like. If an EU law is introduced, and the people of Europe are united against it and elect MEPs to repeal that law. Those MEPs can do nothing about it because they do not have law-making power in the EU. All such power is vested in the commissioners.

In this regard the EU is fundamentally undemocratic. If it completes its transformation into the European superstate, it will not be a democratic superstate like the United States, it will be an authoritarian regime.

Except that what-if scenario doesn't take into consideration the direction of movement in the EU. It is only relatively recently that the parliament had the power of veto, logic dictates that more powers are going to be forthcoming.

And in the meantime, we are left with laws passed before that parliament veto was available, without any democratic recourse to repeal.

War and Peace

Leave

Remain

There certainly hasn't been a European war since World War Two.

Apart from Yugoslavia, Moldova, Cyprus, Ukraine and perhaps a few others.

But they don't count as none of them involved an EU state. No war has ever occurred between any two EU members! Rejoice!

Except that for most of that time the USSR was on Europe's doorstep acting as one very effective unifier.

Except that like-minded western nations don't tend to go to war with each other. Leaving the EU won't change the fact that we are generally allied with the French and think along the same broad lines as the Germans and the rest of the EU. We won't start a war with them and they won't start a war with us.

With one possible exception.

I have personally witnessed an aggressive act by a naval vessel of another EU country against Britain. I was on a boat when a small, but armed, Spanish warship rushed by us at high speed. This was not a permissible incursion and police boats were sent out. It is a frequent occurrence in the seas off Gibraltar. This is not peaceful behaviour between countries but aggressive posturing.

Whether a war starts or not shall be decided by us and them alone. The EU will have nothing to do with it. Witnessing the Spanish behaviour, I am sure that our advanced military is the reason things haven't escalated, in spite of their current actions and the odd comment from locals that we should "blow one of their gunboats out of the water".

I do find the argument that the EU is some sort of great keeper of the peace a rather thin one. In fact, it might be quite the contrary.

There is a school of thought that active EU expansion into the east pushed the Ukraine to its current war.

I don't believe this though. Having been to the Ukraine and seen the locals' attitudes to their neighbours first hand, and the way they are treated by the EU, I'm convinced that the cause of this war is Russian expansionism, not that of the EU.

Although the passive enticing of Ukraine didn't exactly help matters, and is not the behaviour of a great guardian of peace.

Not that I have ever bought into the idea of the EU being some guardian of peace or custodian of international harmony. It is a myth. It is not a reason to stay.

But it is not a reason to leave either. Just because something is a myth, doesn't make the reality behind the myth inherently bad.

Collective Action

Leave

Remain

This is one of the real potential strengths of the EU. 28 countries acting as one toward a common goal. This was put to the test recently with the Russian invasion and annexation of Crimea. The EU was united in opposition to Russian aggression and acted as one by putting sanctions on Russia.

But those sanctions are weak and feeble after national leaders watered down the sanctions so they wouldn't have too great an adverse effect on their own individual trade or interests.

Whilst the action is collective, the result is similar to 28 different countries acting individually. Germany has proved itself to be dependent on Russia for fuel, probably resulting from their unilateral knee-jerk reaction to abolish nuclear power a few years ago. It is the Germans who destroyed their own ability to weather Russian sanctions and made the EU less self-sufficient. They watered down the sanctions and have proved EU collective action to be simply the lowest common denominator.

Had the EU acted decisively, by halting all purchase of Russian fuel, and looked to within and to its allies to keep the lights on, then it would have proven its power and resolve. Instead, it baited the Ukraine and then abandoned her in a very short-sighted, selfish way.

It is akin to the British and French abandoning Czechoslovakia regarding the Sudetenland before the Second World War. To present oneself as a friend and then walk away like that is despicable! It is something I do not want to be associated with.

So, when it comes down to it, the EU is divided. It still acts as a group of selfish individual short-termist nations who are kidding themselves that they're something greater.

And yet, the image of one bloc acting in unison gives us strength. If we are wronged, the EU might react, is a mighty deterrent.

There are also other forms of collective action that benefit us all. Microsoft was reined in by the EU commission, the mighty bloc of nations could stand up to international corporations where individual countries might not be able to.

If national interests diverge then the EU might not act as one, but when they converge, the EU gives yet more strength to their resolve. It supports the smaller nations from bullying by big countries or big business.

Its failures do not dent its potential.

Convention of Human Rights

Leave

Remain

The European Convention of Human Rights has nothing to do with it.

Theresa May mooted a withdrawal from this instead of leaving the EU. Is she absolutely bonkers?

Even Russia is a member of this convention. If a regime as authoritarian as Putin's Russia can meet the requirements of the European Convention of Human Rights then so can we. Even if the Russians cannot, the UK, as a leading world power, and as a democracy, can and should always abide by this convention.

Withdrawing from the convention might see us kicked out of the EU anyway.

Opposing Mrs May may be seen as a reason to vote out in itself! It might even be that our membership of the convention is more at risk if we stay than if we leave.

Immigration

Leave

Remain

I do not accept hands down that too many Europeans are coming here. A lot are, but they are taking up jobs which are available. If British workers are losing out on jobs because of it, then it's probably their fault. The advantage of language, locality *etc* already tips the balance in favour of the Brit.

Those coming to the UK to sponge off our benefits system will no longer be a significant problem following the reforms negotiated by David Cameron. The Prime Minister didn't get much, but he did get that.

I am relaxed about immigration.

But I only see my own narrow world where EU immigrants are decent, hard-working people committed to contributing to British society and building an honest life for themselves.

For whatever reason (house prices, unemployment, evil Romanian gangs *etc*) immigration is deemed too high by the government and they want to reduce it. They have failed, partially because of the EU's free movement of people and labour.

Immigration in other areas could soon become too low. The government's attempts to reduce the arbitrary immigration figure has seen massive crackdowns on non-EU immigration because that is all they can do.

This came home to me when they started targeting genuine international students. When harming our universities is needed to bring the immigration figure down because EU immigration can't be stopped, something is wrong.

But regardless of whether EU immigration is negatively affecting non-EU immigration, regardless of whether it is good or bad, regardless of whether it is too high, I think the decision should be a UK one. If the government wants all Italians to apply for a visa before coming here, or for all Croatians to register online prior to arrival, or restrict Latvians to 3 months without a visa, Westminster should be able to make that decision.

Right now, we cannot stop EU criminals from entering, we aren't even told about criminal records.

We can kick EU nationals out for a select few reasons, vagrancy being one.

But in general, HM Government's hands are tied by the EU.

Say, for example, Slovenia was short of funds and, in order to swell the coffers, the Slovene government allowed anyone in the world to effectively buy Slovenian citizenship. Those who purchased citizenship will suddenly have the right to live in the UK.

I think the EU does have some rules against that…

…but a few crafty lawyers could probably find a loophole.

But let's assume for a moment that they can't, let's assume that the EU legislation is water-tight. That means we will probably be forbidden from granting people citizenship when we want to.

But we definitely *do* have that power under the current system. We granted the citizens of Bermuda, the Cayman Islands and many other territories full British citizenship in 2002. So, this should not be a concern.

Except that proves that any extant EU restrictions are not water-tight. It is possible for a member state to unilaterally change their citizenship law in such a way. Overnight, 150,000 people suddenly gained the right to live and work in Germany, France and any other EEA country, without any of those nations being given an opportunity to voice dissent.

Regardless of what I think about the short-term policies of the government (I support-ed the 2002 act and would expect any equi-valent act in the EU to be for similarly good reasons), it is wrong for a country to not have control of its borders in such a way.

I am confident that I will be able to visit EU countries unimpeded if we leave, I need travel insurance for the EU now, even though I also carry a European Health Ins-urance Card. I am confident that all EU nationals will be able to visit the UK if we leave. This won't change in the slightest.

Yes, we could insist that the Portuguese require visas, as it will be Westminster's decision, but we won't.

I am also sure that EU nationals living in this country will all be allowed to stay. We will not deport people who are here legally.

Irish citizens would still be covered by the terms of the Common Travel Area, which was established in 1923. We didn't with-draw from that when German spies were using it to their advantage during the Sec-ond World War and we won't withdraw from it now.

Even if non-Irish EU nationals who are currently working here are required to have a work visa after a Brexit, they will be able to stay in the UK because already being gainfully employed will make it a near cer-tainty that they can get one. Not that I expect any EU national currently here to need a visa at all.

I do not believe that anyone exercising EU treaty rights in the UK will be deported. I do not have to fear that my EU friends and family will not be welcome here anymore. It just won't happen.

But I shall be disadvantaged if I want to go to Denmark to get a job after an exit.

Disadvantaged, but not disenfranchised. I can still get a work visa.

I've just come back from holiday in the Channel Islands. It was not a foreign holiday; I was still within the British realm. But if I wanted to stay and settle there, or find a job, then tough luck! I would be disappointed.

I'm not entitled to work there or even stay there for longer than 3 months. Yet they're still British. The idea that total unabated free movement of people is required for European cooperation is just wrong. A single sovereign entity does not even need it.

There is a risk that a new land frontier will appear between the EU and the UK on the island of Ireland. The near-invisible border of the present might disappear and check posts might reappear between the North and the South.

Except I don't think it will. Ireland isn't in the Schengen Zone and so the Anglo-Irish land border won't become a covert way to enter the European core. The Republic of Ireland is in the Common Travel Area, as are the non-EU Crown Dependencies.

Travel to and from those places are not impeded. Travelling from a non-EU North and an EU South should be no different than travel from the Isle of Man to the UK or Ireland is at the moment.

Although, it must be said that such controls can be focussed on ports when it is concerning islands. When that new EU border spans across land and splits asunder the maze of roads that crisscross the North-South divide, there might be some unforeseen effect on local people.

Trade

Leave

Remain

Forty something percent of our trade is with the EU, so leaving will hit trade as tariffs are introduced. This is a good short-term reason to stay.

That means of course that over half of our trade is with non-EU countries.

But that isn't up for debate here. Trade with non-EU countries will carry on unaffected by Brexit. The trade with EU countries will be negatively affected and that is a reason to stay.

I have no doubt that we, or any country, would find new trade routes as well as make the existing ones work in the long term. Whether they are the equal of today is another question.

I do not believe that we'll be able to negotiate a special deal with the EU on trade that some Brexit campaigners are suggesting. We might be able to negotiate something to facilitate European trade, but it won't be quick and it won't match actually being in the EU.

I know that *the Economist* ranks Britain top in the world for soft power, but that doesn't necessarily translate into successful trade negotiations with other powerful entities.

However, since net contributions to the EU are larger than the tariffs we would have to pay on EU trade if we fail to negotiate anything (*i.e.* using WTO rules), this isn't as concerning as it sounds.

I am not convinced that so much of our trade should be with Europe anyway. Why should a rich first-world country mainly trade with other rich first-world countries? I am generally in favour of much more extensive trade with emerging Commonwealth economies such as Ghana and Kenya, with whom we have much in common, and other emerging economies such as those of central America, with whom we have little in common, but who will benefit from our custom.

The benefits of trading with such countries will be the enrichment of those places through lawful means (*i.e.* sans narcotics) and do more to further global wellbeing than the EU currently achieves by maintaining selfish and insular policies such as the Common Agricultural Policy.

The development of third-world economies through trade is only impeded by EU protectionism.

There is also the historical factor here. I have neither forgotten nor forgiven the EEC's rôle in destroying trade with New Zealand, Australia and the rest of the Commonwealth.

But I recognise that we cannot bank on those trade routes still being open to us. The fact that membership has been so harmful to our trade in the past, even though it might be beneficial now, is not lost on me. But the past is not a reason to leave. The vote to leave is not a time machine and will not right past wrongs.

Some Commonwealth countries are in the midst of negotiating free-trade arrangements with the EU. Our continued membership might be beneficial for them, perhaps even crucial.

For the world and probably most of the Commonwealth, the UK leaving would be beneficial for their trade. Those arguments do count for something.

But I am unconvinced it is best for our own trade. It will depend on how we adapt to life in the wider international community, and how well we take advantage of having the freedom to trade with the world.

The risk is that, in attempting to become a great trading nation once again, we find ourselves pushed around by China, unable to readapt our economy to our newfound reality.

It is a big world out there, and being the 4th largest economy in the world, as Daniel Hannan is so keen on pointing out, does not give us immunity from the bullish tactics of the second largest or other blocs. Being in the EU, to some degree, does.

Sovereignty

Leave

Remain

A sovereign nation has control over defence and foreign policy. Those are the two crucial elements, and we do have control over them. We have treaties, but these are instruments of policy and do not impede sovereignty. We are a member of Nato; no-one suggests being so makes us less of an independent country. When we went to war in Iraq, France opposed it. Yet we're both in Nato, and both in the EU.

We do not have sovereignty over trade. That is dealt with collectively in the EU, by a single EU representative to the WTO. If we wanted to negotiate trade with India, we can only do so as part of the greater EU.

We do not have sovereignty over our fishing grounds, which are allocated centrally by the EU.

We do not have sovereignty over much of our own law, which can be overridden by a law created by unelected commissioners and reviewed collectively by the whole EU parliament, with scant regard for British individual circumstances.

We can't even choose the colour of our own passports.

I am all for political union. I defended it to the hilt during the Scottish referendum and don't see any problem with it being extended elsewhere.

But local laws must be made locally, just as Scottish law differs from English and Welsh law. Some centralisation can occur, but only when suitable to all parties or crucial to the interests of the whole union.

The USA is an example of good political union. The EU could be that, for the benefit of all, including the British.

But look at the US, individual states control whether it is illegal not to wear a seatbelt! They don't have such minutiae dictated down from on-high.

If another state wants to enter into political union with the UK, I will support it on three conditions, our foreign policy is aligned, our defence policy is aligned and, most importantly, our sovereign is sovereign. Everything else can be devolved.

The EU is almost the polar opposite. Our foreign policy is not aligned, our defence is not aligned, our sovereign is not sovereign yet local laws and regulations are imposed upon us.

Moreover, these laws are not created by our elected representatives in the EU parliament, they are passed down by the unelected bureaucrats of the commission. The parliament recently was allowed to review and veto new laws, but they aren't allowed to make them. And even if they were, it would still be a case of the *two wolves and one sheep voting on lunch* style democracy which will no-doubt be against Britain's interests.

We have found ourselves in the situation where the population is protesting against a tax policy – the *Tampon Tax*, the government willing and keen to abolish it, yet because of EU rules, we are unable to do anything about it.

We can petition the EU to change it.

But all 28 nations would need to agree to the change. In fact, it is even worse than that, with often sub-national legislative bodies wielding an effective veto. Why on earth is it so centralised, and so hard to change things?

Not that is easy to change things in Westminster…

…and yet it is Westminster's desired change that is blocked by the bloc.

The *Tampon Tax* is something which could easily be devolved to regional administrations within the UK, there is no logical reason for it to be centrally controlled. This demonstrates all that is wrong with EU control over our everyday lives, and the impotence of the UK government to implement the will of the British people in what is a wholly good and just cause.

So, I must conclude that we are a client state of a growing European superstate. A superstate that has much of the powers of a state, the legal personality to conduct treaty negotiations on behalf of us, the legal power to make laws which are senior to our laws. The state has all the trimmings too, a flag, an anthem, a president, a parliament, a capital, a currency. This embryonic country is also the imperial overseer of member states, and has exercised its imperial rule by removing the democratically elected governments of Italy and Greece, and exercises less severe punitive measures on a regular basis.

But still we have primary control over our foreign and defence policy, the main bulwarks of our sovereignty.

Our foreign policy is British policy and our armed forces swear allegiance to Her Majesty.

But we know those areas are also in the sights of the EU, with the furthering of the Common Security and Defence Policy, enshrined in the Treaty of Lisbon, to pave the way for an EU Army. This is extremely worrying.

It might be preventable…

…but it is still extremely worrying.

Would the Falklands have been liberated by the EU, or could Spain have vetoed the deployment? Would the EU Army have come to the aid of our allies in Oman, or would Germany have blocked it because of some petty domestic politics? Would they have rescued hostages in Sierra Leone, or would the international bureaucracy have delayed for too long? What would happen if the troubles started again in Northern Ireland? Who would be the commander in chief?

These questions are not ones that face us now...

...but the direction of movement is clearly going down that path.

But, for the moment, British forces serve the Crown and are independent of the EU, and we will be able to steer the EU away from military harmonisation if we are in.

We still have our sovereignty...

...at its most basic. It is severely watered down and under critical and imminent threat from the EU.

The answer to similar criticism in the UK is to slowly devolve more powers to Holyrood, Stormont and the Senedd. The EU answer is, always and unrelentingly, for "more Europe".

Science

Leave

Remain

Scientific research is another area where the EU is beneficial. By pooling scientific resources from all countries, you have a greater range of talent which can be applied in a more efficient way. EU researchers can investigate British problems and British researchers can likewise apply their skills in mainland Europe.

It is a case of everyone wins, a classic instance of us being better than the sum of our parts.

My only grievance would be the amount of influence the EU commissioners have on the areas of research, which I understand to be rather high.

But without knowing more about how it works or knowing of any examples of incompetence, I can only look upon this as a good thing.

I'm also unaware of British science being negatively curtailed by membership. If anything, the influx of European scientists to work in British institutions is a great benefit to our institutions as a whole, thus beneficial for British science in general. The opportunity for British scientists to work throughout Europe is also beneficial.

Of course, I'd like scientists from the world over to be able to work in our institutions and for our scientists to have access to the whole world, if Science Europe is preventing this, then that can surely be the only criticism.

I don't think Science Europe is preventing any such collaboration.

Even if I had disdain for Science Europe, which I do not, that would not be a reason to leave. Such large bodies have to balance many competing economic, social and political factors and to replace the EU body with a British one would not escape those considerations.

History

Leave

Remain

"If we leave the EU, we will go back to the glory days of empire."

It is never said, but hinted at ever so subtly by arch-leavers. This is bollocks!

We may have once been centre of a very successful political union which covered a quarter of the globe and ruled a third of its people, but it's called *history* for a reason. It isn't the case anymore and leaving the EU won't make the slightest bit of difference.

Indeed, you could argue that imperialists who hark back to the glory days of empire should embrace the imperialist centralised nature of the European Union.

But from a historical point of view, our great imperial family was split asunder fighting two world wars to keep Europe free of authoritarian domination. Perhaps we shouldn't have bothered. Perhaps we should have let Austria-Hungary and Germany dominate the mainland, saved our empire, prevented the rise of national socialism and resulted in a very similar looking unified Europe.

Ah! Alternative history, utter bollocks too!

If we leave, we must stand on our credentials as they are today, and as they'll be in the years to come. Initially, we'll have to do this alone. We can learn much from our history, and keep much, but we can't rely on it. The British Empire is a footnote in history and that is the end of it.

But there is more. The fact that people are suggesting we abandon European and international conventions, such as the metric system, and return to a glorious day of Imperial measurements, exposes another risk of leaving. Should such people ever be in a position to act on their fantasies, buoyed by a leave victory, they may well do so and do real harm to the country.

We do not share a currency with Europe, but we do, in the main, share their method of measuring things. In common parlance I am 6'1" tall, I weigh ... um ... several stone and live 40 miles from London. I am not averse to using these measurements, but to return to a world where bags of sugar must be measured in pounds does no-one any favours.

It would make more sense to return to £sd.

Extremism

The far-right are generally in support of an exit. I don't want to share a platform with the far right, so I should vote remain.

But Brexit is not an inherently far-right policy. There is no doubt about that. Should I vote to stay just because my ideological enemies want out?

Maybe I should.

The far-right and hard-left is gaining momentum throughout Europe and in this country, it wasn't that long ago that the BNP had seats in the EU parliament. "Gagged for telling the truth" was their slogan at the time, their election victory sent a shiver down my spine. They should be opposed.

In France the FN is gaining ground on an anti-EU message. Far-right gains in Austria has forced their premier to resign. In Greece both the far-right and hard-left have gained ground in direct response to EU policy in that country.

So, as much as it goes against the European ideal, the principle of democracy and the horrific memory of both fascism and Soviet domination in Europe, it is just possible that the EU is an indirect cause of this troubling phenomenon?

I'm not going to conclude one way or another on this one, nor should I let it affect my vote. We should treat these groups as if they don't exist, and conclude based on the merits of each argument.

Economic Matters

Leave

Remain

Will the UK be richer inside or out? The answer appears to be inside, at least in the short term.

Just like trade, we are interlinked with the EU and leaving will result in a shock to the economy. Fear of the future will cause problems; growth will be reduced. All of this I do believe.

Companies will move out of the UK resulting in job losses, and it might destroy the economic progress we've made so far.

It sounds bad doesn't it, but there are beacons of light: Only 36% of the FTSE 100 openly support remain…

…but none have openly supported leave.

When 63% seem indifferent it starts to lose its terrifying edge.

Then there is HSBC. The bank talked quite seriously about leaving the UK, openly discussing it. It was assumed that this was related to the EU referendum. Yet they have already decided to stay – the advantages of the UK, regardless of EU membership, is clearly beneficial for them. They won't leave.

In the long term, HSBC think the UK will still be okay. Good enough for them to still be here – so it isn't as bad as it sounds, at least for big business. They may want us to stay, but they don't think it will be cataclysmic if we leave.

And suddenly I find myself thinking that something "not being a cataclysm" is a reason to vote leave. It is not. HSBC want us to remain in the EU because it will be beneficial for them. It will be beneficial to a British company; therefore, it will be beneficial to Britain.

British car manufacture is strongly intertwined with the EU, would they leave?

Or would they want to weather the storm and keep their experienced staff. Moving factories is very expensive.

But having a factory outside the EU might be even more costly. All those parts flowing seamlessly across the border from Britain to the mainland and back again, that can't be unaffected by a leave vote, can it?

The most successful investor in the world – Warren Buffett – says he hopes we stay in.

He also doesn't think that an exit will make any difference to the financial markets, and he won't change "one iota of what he is doing in businesses or stocks".

Another opinion is that the UK could be seen as a safer haven against the chaos in the EU if we leave.

Not that I believe that. A Brexit will cause enough chaos in the UK to offset any benefit like that.

What about small businesses? The deregulation of the EU will make things easier for them, right?

Except I don't believe massive deregulation will happen. If we want to continue to trade with the EU, which we do, then we will have to abide by EU regulations; not all of them, but a lot. So the benefits here are limited.

Some of the regulation is British anyway, such as holiday pay, and the likelihood is that many (probably most) of the EU-originated regulations will remain, because they are good. So the changes will be few.

Of course, that could be a reason to leave as well. We won't be abandoning those good regulations that we rely on day-to-day.

But they will be less secure.

The bad regulations, of which I do not doubt there are many, can be got rid of.

I wonder how long that'll take. I wonder if it is easy to tell the good from the bad.

Ignoring all of that. It seems that general consensus is that things will be worse for big business...

...and better for small business.

If you are pro-big business, then vote in.

If you are pro-small business, then vote out.

It can't be that simple though. Can it? I'm just not suited to fully understand these arguments.

Then it comes to steel.

Chinese economic tactics have attacked British steel and almost killed it, it looks like it will struggle on, but at the cost of many jobs and pay rates. The EU failed us.

Would the UK government have acted decisively and successfully in protecting our steel industry against Chinese aggression? I'm afraid I don't think it would have either.

But the EU actually failed us, whereas I'm just guessing the UK authorities would have done.

Affiliation with Other EU Nations

Leave

Remain

I look at the other member states and, in general, I like them. I like being associated with them and actually feel an affectionate connection to all of them bar one.

Whilst I like being a member of a club with my friends, if the club is rubbish, being in it with your friends is scant consolation.

The UK has more in common with a great many countries around the world than it does with the countries of the EU. The Commonwealth is family…

…the EU nations are friends. There is no reason to leave there.

The bloc is a patchwork of different states with their own culture and traditions.

A cultural patchwork that I feel the EU is destroying, and to leave it might in some indirect way halt this cultural destruction.

But it is such a tenuous link that I will not let it be a reason to leave.

Being associated with these countries is a definite reason to remain in the EU. I might not like the club itself, but I do like being in a club with my mates.

The Commonwealth and the USA

Leave

Remain

If it is in the interest of the USA to stay in the EU, then that alone is a good reason to stay.

A member of the Australian parliament recently spoke at how the UK should leave, and that whilst having UK influence in the EU was somewhat beneficial to Australia, the price we are paying is far too high and that Australia should support us should we decide to leave.

But as demonstrated by this, we are beneficial to Australia by being in, and that alone is another good reason to stay.

If we do decide to leave, I have no doubt that America and Australia will support us insofar as it is in their interest (in spite of "back of the queue" comments).

That is to be welcomed, and goes some way to dispelling my fear of leaving, but it is not a reason to leave – supporting our Commonwealth family by staying is a reason to stay.

Future

Leave

Remain

When I think of life in the EU, and how the country will look going forward, I see a European United States, a monotonous entity which may or may not have solved its current animosity towards democracy. I see our country being a province of the greater state, nothing more. I see our monarch becoming a sub-national monarch like the King of Hawaii or of the Ashanti. It is bleak.

When I think of life out of the EU, and how the country will look should we leave, I do not see a land of milk and honey. We could genuinely become an insular inward-looking country, but I doubt that. More likely is that the economic shock will harm us irreparably, and we will look back upon EU membership as we now look back on the Victorian era: "Britain was powerful then".

But I also see possibility. Such as the reopening of worldwide trade routes and the increased investment and support for developing countries. We could even enter a new political union with a more suited country, not creating the autocratic, bureaucratic, centralised, authoritarian monster that blends Europe together like an international smoothie, with scant regard for the culture or traditions of member states that we have today, but a peaceful harmonious union between countries that respect each other's uniqueness and where no-one feels trapped.

And yet, that is fantastical. It is unrealistic.

And yet, is it not worth aiming for the stars?

In essence, I see hope without the EU, hopelessness within.

So, shall I vote with my heart, rather than my head? But even then, my heart yearns to be with my EU friends. When your heart and your head tell you the same thing, surely you must agree. Remain with our friends.

Friends together, in chains.

But what happens to the rest of Europe should we leave? Would the EU break up?

It might.

There are already murmurings from the Czechs. The Dutch have expressed their displeasure. In France the FN are gaining ground on their Eurosceptic credentials (if it's for any other reason, the French are in trouble). Should we stay and support the call for change in the EU? Yanis Varoufakis thinks we should. He is no friend of the EU, but he thinks it is worth sticking together.

When voting for a group like the FN is seen as a legitimate way, indeed, the only way, to protest against the EU, feelings must be running quite high. Luckily, we have UKIP, an alternative to the BNP. Nick Griffin might well have won the elections in 2014 were it not for Nigel Farage!

I see a few possibilities:

Maybe our leaving will kick the EU into real actual reform. Ironic that we won't be in to benefit from it.

Maybe our leaving will encourage a select few others to leave, Denmark and Sweden perhaps, maybe the Czechs, but no Eurozone members and the bloc survives.

Maybe the bloc will fail, but so tight is the economic grip on most member states that it will soldier on in some form.

I see a few more possibilities, such as north-south splits, but I don't think the whole thing will go back to not existing.

None of these are really cataclysmic. I don't foresee a war ravaging Europe. I don't see intra-European cold war. I don't even see us becoming unfriendly towards our former EU partners. They'll still be friends.

If we don't leave, I think things will continue pretty much as they are for a while. But if the EU doesn't reform, I see something akin to the troubles in Northern Ireland flaring up. Not here, probably in Greece or Italy, or somewhere else that has suffered an assault on their democracy from the EU.

Conclusions

Leave   ## Remain

When I started writing down my thoughts on this, I thought that I'd conclude that the arguments are finely balanced. And indeed, it is a difficult decision.

There are indeed very good reasons to stay...

...and very good reasons to go.

The EU is a fundamentally undemocratic institution...

...but its powers over us aren't absolute.

We do have some major influence and our economy has been intertwined with Europe over the last 40 years. Perhaps in hindsight we should never have joined, but it is too late to leave now.

Except that the future in the EU looks so bleak. We're heading into being a province of a superstate, where our culture and ideals will be eroded away along with our sovereignty. Leaving won't be pleasant, but perhaps it's worth it.

Except that livelihoods are on the line. Prices will change and we shall be poorer if we go. I am alright, but there are many who aren't as fortunate as me. Is it worth the risk to avoid a superstate that might not ever emerge?

Except that when the most successful investor in the world doesn't think it'll make him invest differently; the economic shock is unlikely to be that great.

Then there's the young. My children will be robbed of the option to go into the heart of Europe to find a job and an adventure.

But at least they won't be robbed of their culture or identity.

I have tried to analyse everything as much as one man can, not everything is equal, some matters are more important than others.

The cost of EU membership is exceedingly high, both in terms of money and in terms of freedom. The sovereignty and democracy arguments are epic and central.

The cost of leaving is potentially very high, we shall lose influence, and lose very beneficial cooperation in numerous areas. We could lose a great deal of money.

It isn't an easy decision to make, but this exercise will have helped me make it.

When I eventually make it.

Where will I put that damned ×?

Referendum on the United Kingdom's membership of the European Union	**2016**
Vote only once by putting a cross **X** in the box next to your choice	
Should the United Kingdom remain a member of the European Union or leave the European Union?	
Remain a member of the European Union	☐
Leave the European Union	☐

And thus lives are changed.